Thistle Starts Exploring

Lady Thistle, the Horse

D.H. ANDERSON
Illustrations by STEVEN LESTER

Thistle Starts Exploring

Paperback ISBN 978-1-960007-15-5
HardBack ISBN 978-1-960007-14-8
eBOOK ISBN 978-1-960007-16-2

Published by
Little Blessing Books
an imprint of
Orison Publishers, Inc.
PO Box 188, Grantham, PA 17027
www.OrisonPublishers.com

Acknowledgments

Contributing Artist: A. Newman
Contributing Veterinarian: Apryle Horbal, VMD

Just a few nights ago, a baby horse was born at Waterdam Farm. Her name is Lady Thistle. Her mother, Polly, and her whole human family are happy. But dangers lurk for baby horses, and everyone wants Thistle to be safe as she starts to explore her world.

First, Thistle learns how to nurse. Polly shows her how to stand to drink her milk. Milk is a baby horse's only food, and it is important for Thistle to nurse often, so her bones and muscles grow big and strong.

Thistle is now quite good at getting up and moving about the stall, and she is better at balancing on her long legs. She looks at the grain in the feeder, watches her mother nibble, and touches the cool, fresh water with her curious nose. It tickles!

But she does not know how to eat grain or drink from the water bucket...*yet!*

She and Polly are comfortable when their human family visits. They allow Dr. Apryle to check on them each day. But the farmhands must be extra careful when they enter the stall to clean or to place food and water there for Polly. Thistle is very curious. When someone visits, she tries to get out!

One morning, Thistle awakes, ready to nurse. But Polly is not paying attention to her baby; instead, she is happily licking something hanging from the wall. Thistle watches Polly's long, pink tongue and nickers, wondering what could be so enjoyable.

Polly nickers back, "Come see."

Thistle stands and wobbles over. She wants to try. But where is her tongue? How does she use it? Then, nature takes over, and Thistle reaches up and licks.

MMMMMMMMM! A salt block!

The family places a stall guard across Polly's stall door so the mom and baby can look out into the aisle. Thistle is not afraid to put her nose out, and she gets a good look at the other horses, who stretch their necks to look at her.

Wynter, the grumpy old horse in the barn, is startled by the tiny creature. But then he sees her with Polly and realizes she is the new baby everyone has been waiting for.

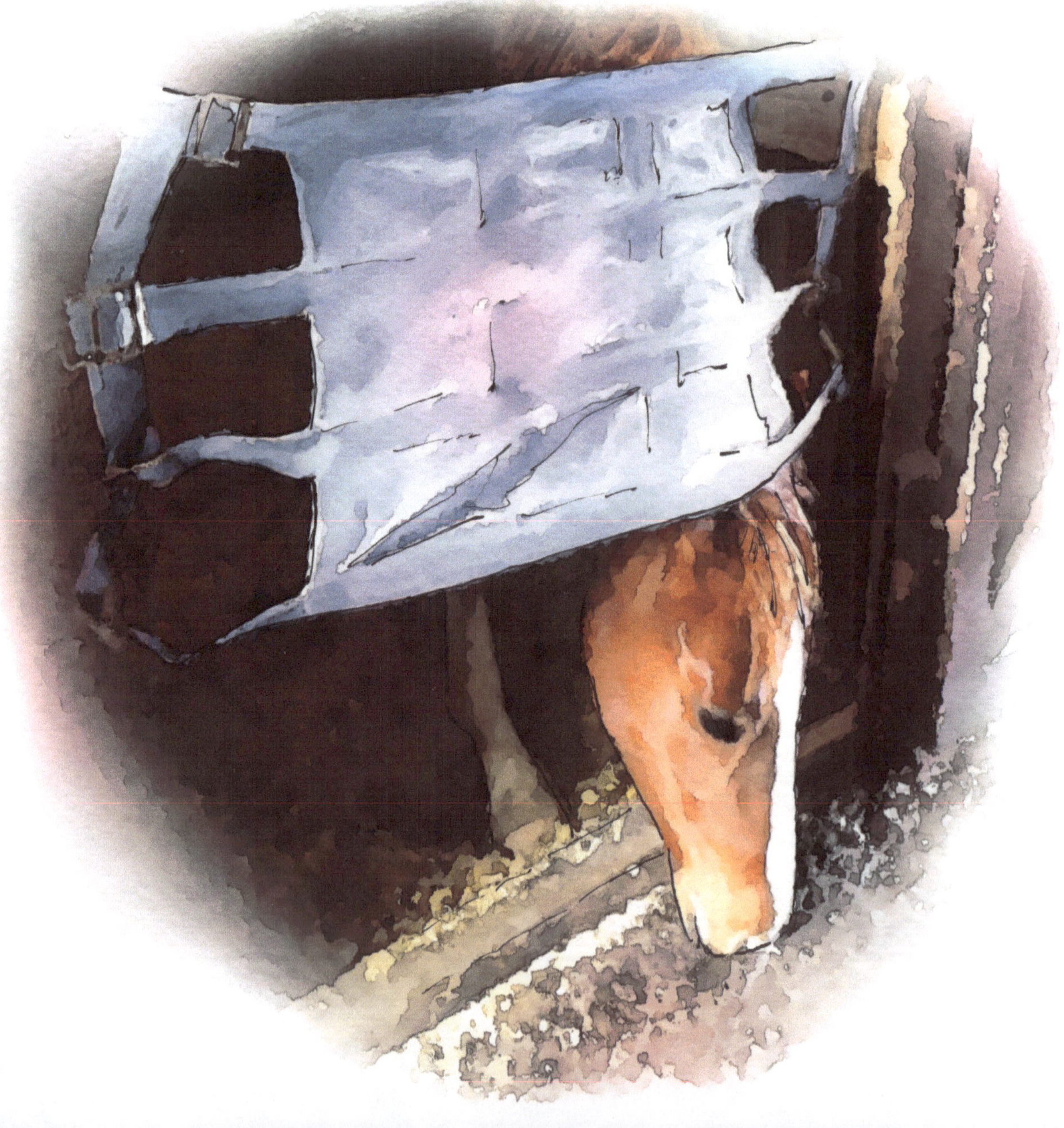

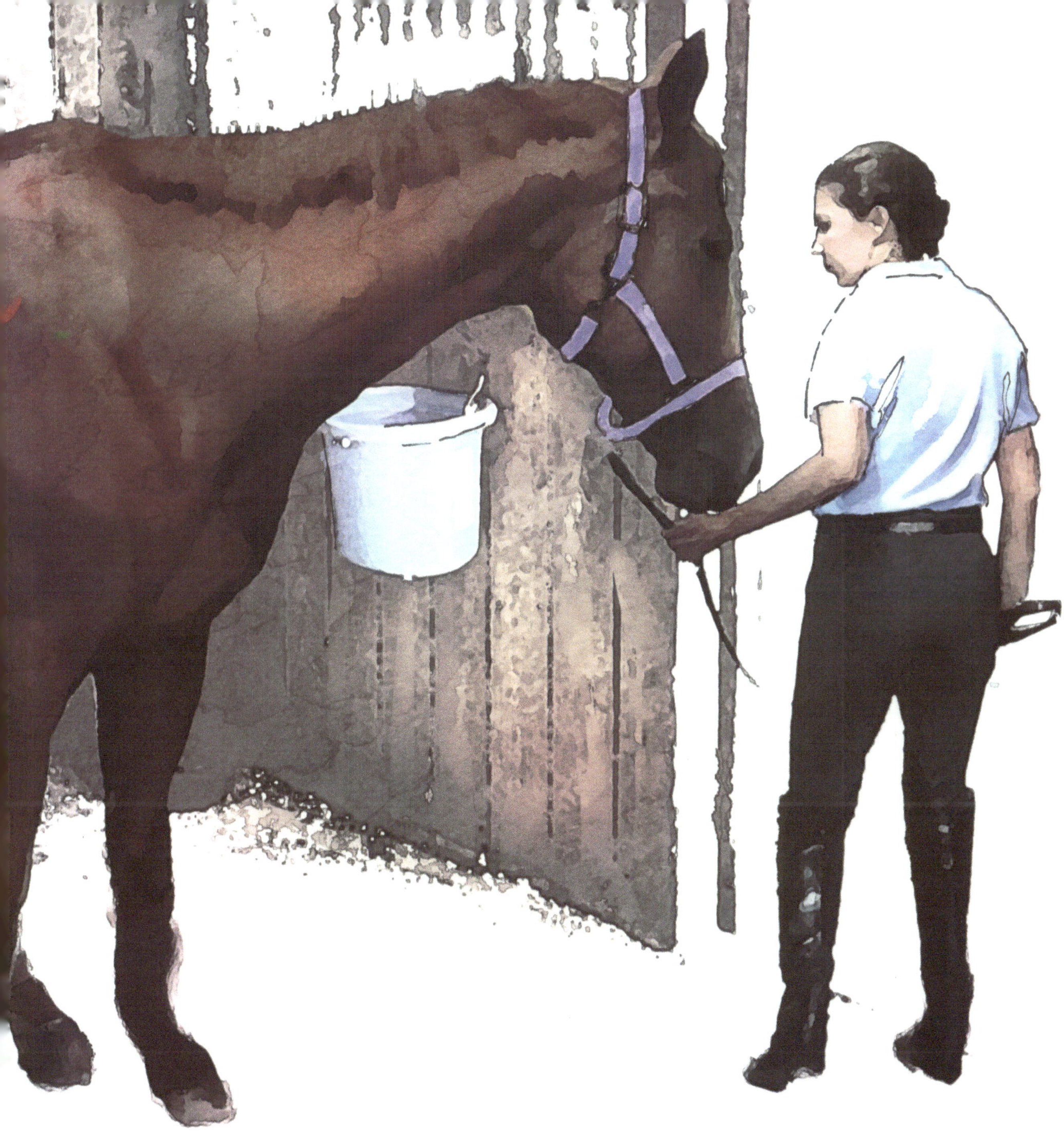

Each day, Thistle nurses and grows bigger and stronger. When she is five days old, her human family thinks she is ready for a short walk outside with Polly. Dr. Apryle and Taylor place a halter on Polly, who has worn a halter many times. Thistle cannot wear a halter around her delicate, newborn neck.

They are ready to lead Polly out the stall door.

Thistle is worried. She wants to stay close to Polly, but she is afraid to leave home.

Polly nickers, telling Thistle that she will be safe, and she leads the way down the aisle and out of the stable.

Thistle sees many new things, like green pastures, and hears new sounds, like birds twittering in the trees as she hobbles along. The path is rocky, but her legs are getting stronger. Wynter and Daphne are watching from their field.

Dr. Apryle decides the walk has been long enough. She turns Polly around, and they head back to the stable. Dr. Apryle and Taylor are happy that Thistle's first walk went well!

The next morning as Thistle nurses, all she can think about is going outside!

She remembers the

trees

swooping birds

flowers

buzzing bees

growling farm machines

leaves rustling in the breeze

A farmhand arrives and puts a lead rope on Polly. She nickers, telling Thistle to stay close as they walk to the pasture . Dr. Apryle and Taylor watch, just to make sure Thistle stays safe. Thistle now eagerly walks to the field, again enjoying the sights and sounds of the farm. Today, she and Polly will stay outside!

When they enter the gate, Polly kicks up her legs and runs. Thistle follows Mom's lead and finds that she, too, loves to run!

They begin a daily routine of going out to the pasture.

Thistle watches Polly drink water, then dips her nose in the water. She sniffs the grass. Her cat friend Freeway comes to the fence to visit, and Thistle reaches under with her nose to greet him. They are both very curious.

Polly enjoys eating grass! Thistle cannot eat the luscious grass yet, so she nurses. Then she lies down in the middle of the pasture for a nap.

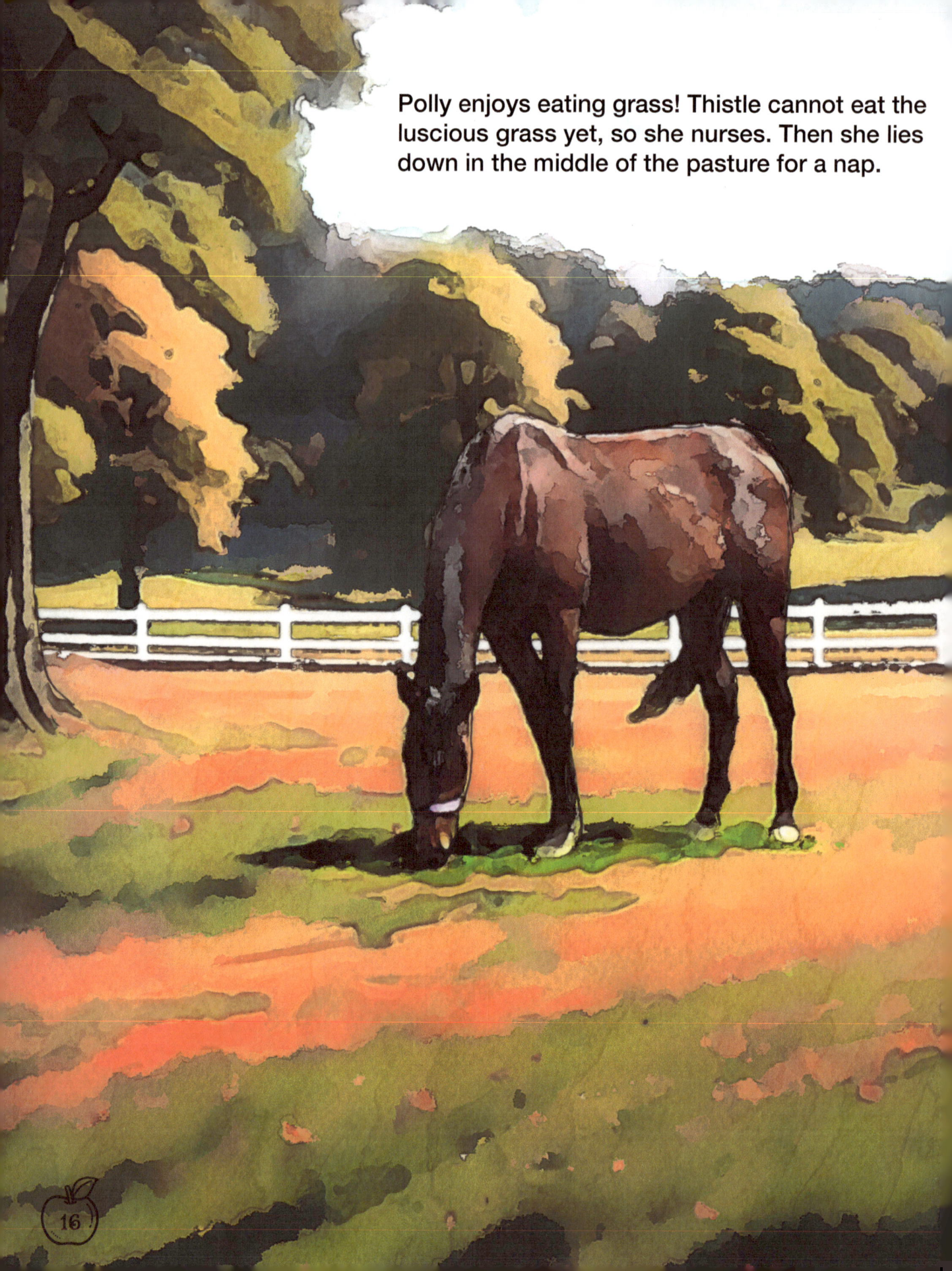

Thistle follows Polly out to their field each
day and then back to the stable at night.

Each day, Thistle becomes even braver and more curious. The farmhands guide her more closely. Polly knows there are dangers and reminds Thistle to stay close..

But one day, Thistle decides it is time to explore. She trots away and does not listen to the farmhands as they try to keep her with Polly.

Polly is upset, but she can't go to Thistle because of her lead rope.
She calls, but her brave little girl does not listen. Thistle is so excited
to be on her own.

Wynter and Daphne are at the fence, watching and wondering what
the little one is doing.

Thistle trots over to visit them. They nuzzle her but then nudge her firmly, telling her to go back to her mom.

Suddenly, Thistle realizes she is not so brave after all, and she trots quickly back to Polly's side. Safe again!

The family decides it may be time for Thistle to wear a halter. Dr. Apryle says Thistle's delicate neck could be injured by a halter if it is pulled too hard. She calls Trainer Blaine, who shows everyone how to use a lead line wrapped around Thistle's chest and hind quarters instead of her neck.

Each day, Thistle and Polly are walked safely to the pasture.

Each evening, all of the horses return to the barn for a rest and their grain!

Thistle is sleepy from learning and growing!

And, once again, the stable is quiet,
except for the soothing munching of hay....

Did You Know...?

Horses live in *herds*—large groups, like extended families. That is how they stay safe. A foal will always want to stay close to its mother. The mare should always be able to see and get to her foal.

Foals have tiny feet and thin legs that get stuck in small spaces like holes. They must be careful where they step because their hooves are soft. Predators, such as wolves, are also a threat to baby horses. It is important for foals to stay close to their mothers and their herds for protection.

Leading a foal requires careful consideration. The foal must trust humans, which it can learn to do in its first hours of life. Even just patting and stroking the foal before it gets up will begin this bond. Then, when it comes time to use a halter or rope, the foal will accept it.

Fields where horses—especially foals—will be grazing need to be checked often for:

- Fences with sharp edges;

- Wire, especially barbed wire—horses often panic if they get caught and fight to get free, which can cause bad injuries;

- Plants that are harmful if they are eaten or touch a horse's skin or hooves. Where Thistle lives, some examples are poison hemlock, buttercups, red maple, and black walnut;

- Clean and plentiful water—no bugs or algae. Water buckets or tubs must be cleaned, and the water must be changed regularly.

A salt block contains sodium chloride and other minerals that horses do not always get enough of in their feed. The amount a horse needs depends on how much it works, because horses lose salt when they sweat. They enjoy licking salt, so care must be taken that they do not get too much.

Coming Soon!

Thistle Gets Hurt

D.H. ANDERSON

Illustrations by STEVEN LESTER

Lady Thistle, the Horse
BOOK FOUR

Watch

for the

Next Book

in the

Series

SCAN ME

Read more stories as young Thistle grows.

www.ingramcontent.com/pod-product-compliance
Lightning Source LLC
Chambersburg PA
CBHW041607120626
46551CB00002B/339